How to Play the Trombone for Beginners

The Ultimate Guide to Learning, Playing, and Becoming Proficient at the Instrument

Table of Contents

Introduction

Have you ever wondered what creating soul-stirring melodies with a trombone feels like? Are you curious about the secrets hidden within this elegant brass instrument?

If so, you're in the right place. "How to Play the Trombone for Beginners " is your ticket to unlocking the captivating world of trombone music. This comprehensive guide takes you from square one, providing a solid foundation that even beginners can quickly grasp. Its mission is to make learning the Trombone easy, enjoyable, and accessible.

What sets this book apart? Whether you're a novice or have some musical experience, it's designed for your needs. Structured into eight chapters, each builds upon the last, ensuring a smooth and engaging learning experience. From diving into the history and background of the Trombone in Chapter 1 to mastering advanced techniques in Chapter 8, you'll find it all.

This book isn't about theory alone but hands-on and practical approaches. You'll discover step-by-step instructions complemented by clear illustrations. They'll guide you through everything from assembling your instrument to producing your first notes. This book breaks down the complexities of embouchure and breath control so you can confidently embark on your journey.

This guide is your mentor, simplifying everything and making it easy to understand. You'll soon be playing simple melodies and, with practice, advancing your skills to become a confident trombonist. So, if you've ever dreamed of making beautiful music with the Trombone, grab your instrument and embark on this exciting journey.

Whether young or young at heart, "How to Play the Trombone for Beginners" is your gateway to the world of music. It invites you to embrace the magic of this remarkable instrument.

Chapter 1: Background to the Trombone

Have you ever wondered what makes the Trombone such a captivating instrument, capable of sending shivers down your spine or making you want to get up and dance? Do you find yourself spellbound by its iconic shape and the glimmer of brass beneath stage lights? If so, you're about to embark on a journey that will satisfy your curiosity and get you playing.

The deep, resonant voice of the Trombone commands attention and stirs emotions. With its iconic slide and brass brilliance, the Trombone has a magnetic quality that has captivated music lovers for centuries.

Exploring the History and Significance of the Trombone in Music

Dating back to the 15th century, the Trombone has a lineage that traverses the annals of time and spans continents, leaving an indelible mark on the world of music. The Trombone's origins can be traced to the sackbut, a precursor that graced the Renaissance era with its melodic presence. However, it wasn't until the 18th century that the modern Trombone, with its iconic slide mechanism, came into its own. This innovation was pivotal in the instrument's evolution, setting the stage for its ascendancy in the music world.

The Trombone's journey of transformation is a resounding testament to human ingenuity. The addition of the slide was nothing short of revolutionary, allowing for a seamless and uninterrupted range of notes. This newfound capability elevated the Trombone to a prominent position within orchestras, where its distinct timbre came to the forefront.

The timbre of the Trombone is unique, characterized by a harmonious blend of warm, mellow tones and bright, piercing accents. This distinctive sonic signature sets it apart from other brass instruments. It has an unmistakable voice that tugs at heartstrings and commands attention with unparalleled authority.

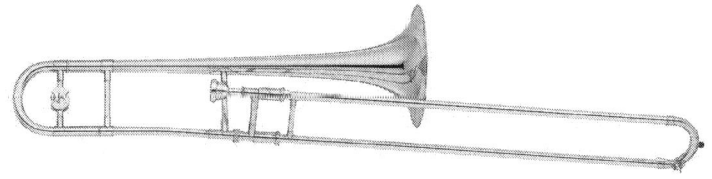

1. *The Trombone is versatile, allowing it to be used in different music genres and contexts. Source: Yamaha Corporation, CC BY-SA 4.0 <https://creativecommons.org/licenses/by-sa/4.0>, via Wikimedia Commons: https://commons.wikimedia.org/wiki/File:Yamaha_Tenor_tromb one_YSL-891Z_(re-crop).jpg*

Yet, what truly sets the Trombone apart is its remarkable versatility. It possesses the rare ability to adapt to an astonishing array of musical genres and contexts. From the soaring solos that transport listeners to ethereal realms to the foundational bassline in an ensemble, the Trombone is a virtuoso of musical flexibility.

The Trombone's adaptability has earned it a place of honor in both classical and contemporary compositions, transcending eras and genres. It stands as a testament to the enduring allure of this instrument, which continues to inspire musicians and capture the hearts of audiences worldwide. So, as you journey deeper into the world of trombone playing, remember that you are stepping into a tradition that spans centuries, guided by an instrument as versatile as it is enchanting.

Understanding the Role of the Trombone in Various Genres

The Trombone adds gravitas to symphonies in classical music, casting a spell with its majestic sound. Composers like Richard Wagner and Gustav Mahler harnessed this instrument's power to evoke deep emotions and grandeur in their compositions. In the hands of a skilled trombonist, this instrument sends music straight into the listener's soul.

In jazz, the trombone swings and improvises, showcasing its playful side. Legends like J.J. Johnson and Tommy Dorsey have paved the way for modern jazz trombonists, pushing the boundaries of what's possible with this instrument. Its unique ability to produce glissandos (smooth slides between notes) adds a layer of expressiveness that jazz musicians love.

The Trombone's versatility extends to marching bands, commanding attention, and inspiring parades. Its stately presence and ability to cut through the noise of a bustling parade make it a vital ensemble component. From the lively streets of New Orleans to the grandeur of Macy's Thanksgiving Day Parade, the Trombone's role is indispensable.

In popular music, the Trombone has featured prominently in rock 'n' roll, funk, and soul. Think of the unforgettable horn section in classic Motown hits or the iconic riffs in rock anthems. The Trombone's ability to inject soul and energy into any genre is remarkable. It adds a layer of sophistication to funk grooves and brings nostalgia to rock ballads.

Setting Realistic Expectations for the Journey Ahead

Now, as you embark on your trombone journey, it's essential to set realistic expectations. Learning the Trombone is a rewarding but challenging endeavor. Beginners often find comfort in knowing that even the most accomplished trombonists started with the basics. It's a gradual progression, and the key is patience.

Learning to play the Trombone is a journey that offers a world of musical possibilities. However, like any skill, it requires dedication and a realistic understanding of what lies ahead.

The Learning Curve

As a beginner, you won't master the Trombone overnight. Expect to encounter challenges, frustrations, and moments when you question your progress. But remember, these experiences are all part of the learning process. Every accomplished trombonist was once a beginner.

Practice Makes Perfect

To make steady strides, commit to a regular practice schedule. Aim for daily practice sessions, even if they are short. Consistency is key. As you practice, you'll gradually develop muscle memory and improve your tone, technique, and overall playing ability.

Setting Realistic Goals

One way to stay motivated is by setting realistic short-term and long-term goals. Short-term goals may include mastering a particular scale or improving your articulation. Long-term goals could involve performing a solo piece or joining a local ensemble. Having clear goals helps you track your progress and celebrate your achievements.

Seeking Guidance

Don't be afraid to seek guidance from a qualified trombone teacher or mentor. They provide invaluable insights, correct your technique, and offer personalized feedback. A good teacher will help you navigate challenges and tailor lessons to your needs and goals, significantly accelerating your learning curve.

The Importance of Patience

Some techniques will seem elusive at first, but with time and effort, they will become second nature. Avoid the trap of comparing yourself to others, especially more experienced players. Everyone progresses at their own pace, so focus on your growth and enjoy the journey.

Breathing and Posture

Before you even produce a sound on the Trombone, you must understand the importance of proper breathing and posture. How you breathe and hold the instrument significantly impacts your sound quality and overall playing experience. Imagine your body as your instrument's engine. Without proper breathing and posture, your engine won't run smoothly.

Here's a simple step-by-step exercise to help you get started:

1. Stand or sit up straight with your shoulders relaxed.

2. Take a deep breath through your nose, filling your lungs.

3. As you exhale through your mouth, engage your diaphragm and core muscles.

4. Practice this deep breathing technique regularly to build stamina and control.

Embracing Mistakes

Don't get discouraged when you make a mistake while playing the Trombone. Instead, view it as an opportunity to learn and improve. Even professional trombonists make mistakes during performances. The key is how you recover and continue playing.

As you advance, you'll unlock the world of scales, simple melodies, and techniques. These are the building blocks of your musical vocabulary, the words and phrases you'll use to communicate through your Trombone. Remember, every note you play brings you one step closer to mastering this extraordinary instrument. The journey is as beautiful as the destination. So, embrace the journey, and let the Trombone's enchanting call guide you.

Chapter 2: Getting to Know Your Instrument

Before you become a proficient trombonist, it's crucial to establish a strong foundation by knowing your instrument inside and out. Playing trombone music is about more than hitting the right notes. You won't be able to hit the right notes unless you have a functioning trombone. It all begins with knowing the individual parts and how they work together. Once you do, you will better understand how the instrument is played. Confidence doesn't come instantly—it is a gradual process obtained over time, and as you learn about the instrument, you plant the acorn of confidence that will someday grow into a mighty oak.

Familiarizing Yourself with the Different Parts of the Trombone

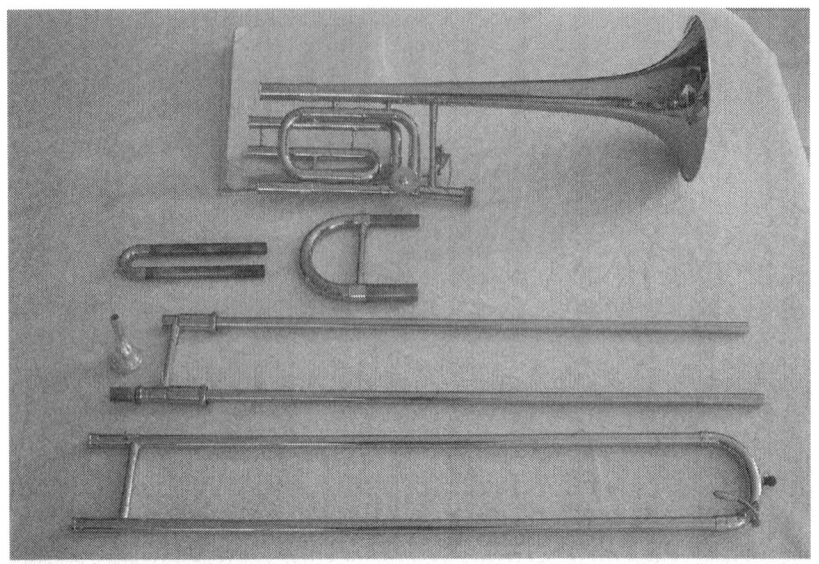

2. *Understanding the anatomy of a trombone can help you master the instrument. Source: Kyx63, CC BY-SA 3.0 <https://creativecommons.org/licenses/by-sa/3.0>, via Wikimedia Commons: https://commons.wikimedia.org/wiki/File:Trombone_d%C3%A9m ont%C3%A9.jpg*

Mastering any musical instrument requires a deep understanding of its anatomy and how each component contributes to its unique sound. The Trombone's rich history and distinctive sound are no exception.

The Bell: Shaping Sound and Projection

The bell of the Trombone is its most recognizable feature—the flared, bell-shaped end. The bell plays a critical role in shaping the instrument's sound.

Sound Resonance: When you blow air into the mouthpiece and buzz your lips, the sound waves travel down the Trombone's tubing and exit through the bell. The size and shape of the bell influence how these sound waves are amplified and projected. A larger bell generally produces a warmer, more resonant sound, while a smaller bell offers a brighter tone.

Projection: The bell's flare also affects the projection of sound. A wide bell can help the sound reach the audience more effectively, making it ideal for playing in larger venues or outdoor settings. Trombonists often use this to their advantage when performing in different spaces.

The Slide: The Heart of the Trombone

The slide is undoubtedly the most iconic and unique feature of the Trombone. It's what allows trombonists to produce different pitches. Mastering its movement is fundamental to playing the instrument.

Pitch Control: The slide consists of two parallel tubes that can be extended or retracted. When you push the slide out, the Trombone produces lower notes, and the pitch becomes higher when you pull it in. This slide mechanism sets the Trombone apart from other brass instruments with valves.

Intonation: Achieving accurate intonation (playing in tune) requires precise slide control. Even a slight variation in slide position will affect the pitch. Regular slide maintenance, including lubrication, ensures smooth and precise movement.

The Mouthpiece Receiver: Shaping Tone and Timbre

The mouthpiece receiver may seem minor, but it plays a significant role in shaping the Trombone's tone and timbre.

Tone Control: The mouthpiece receiver is where you insert the mouthpiece. Different mouthpiece receivers subtly alter the timbre of the instrument. By experimenting with various mouthpiece receivers, trombonists can fine-tune their sound to match their preferences.

Comfort and Playability: The shape and size of the mouthpiece receiver also impact the player's comfort and endurance. A well-matched mouthpiece receiver contributes to a trombonist's overall ease of playing.

The Valve Section (Optional): Changing Pitch without the Slide

While not all trombones have valves, some do, and they offer an alternative way to change the instrument's pitch without moving the slide.

Valve Trombones: Valves are commonly found on valve trombones and work similarly to valves on other brass instruments like trumpets. By depressing specific valves, you change the length of the tubing, altering the pitch.

Versatility: Valve trombones are favored for their ease of use and versatility. They are often chosen for specific musical styles, such as Dixieland jazz, where rapid changes in pitch are common.

The Water Key: Keeping Things Dry

Moisture can accumulate inside the Trombone while playing due to condensation. The water key, typically found on the main tuning slide, is a small but essential feature for maintaining the instrument's performance.

Condensation Release: The water key allows you to release accumulated moisture. Keeping this key functioning correctly prevents water from affecting the Trombone's sound.

The Tuning Slide: Adjusting Overall Pitch

The tuning slide is where you adjust the Trombone's pitch. It's a crucial tool for playing in tune with other instruments and ensuring that your music sounds harmonious.

Pitch Adjustment: By extending or retracting the tuning slide, you change the overall pitch of the instrument. Keep the tuning slide lubricated for smooth adjustments and precise tuning.

Understanding these essential parts of the Trombone is the first step toward becoming a confident and skilled trombonist. Whether you're a beginner or an experienced player, a deeper knowledge of your instrument will enhance your musical journey and allow you to unlock the full potential of the Trombone's unique sound. So, take the time to familiarize yourself with your Trombone's anatomy, and let your musical exploration begin.

The Different Types of Trombones and Their Characteristics

The world of music is as diverse as the instruments that create it. The Trombone comes in various types, each with unique characteristics and applications.

The Tenor Trombone: Versatility Personified

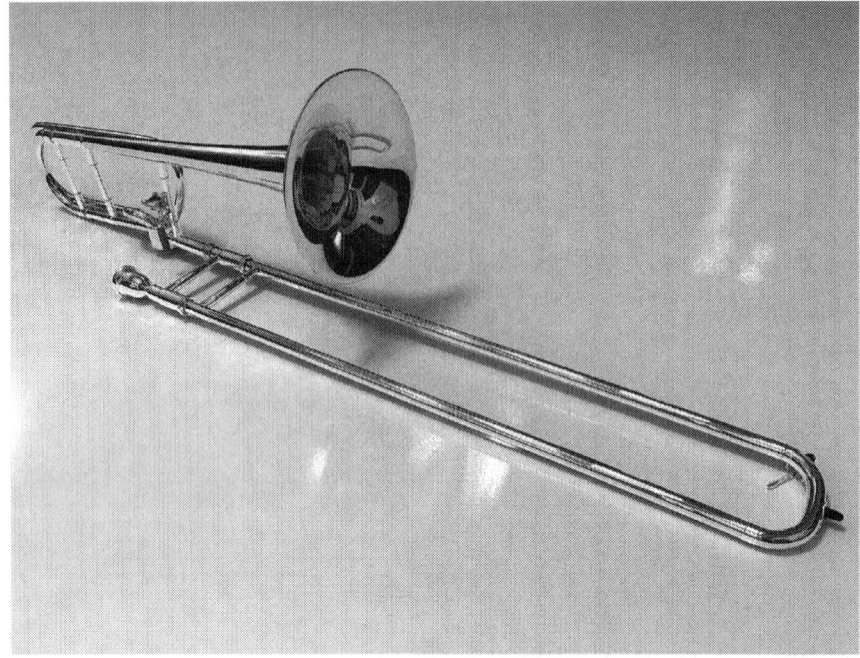

*3. The tenor trombone is the most recognizable type. Source: FlamM,
CC BY-SA 3.0 <http://creativecommons.org/licenses/by-sa/3.0/>,
via Wikimedia Commons:
https://commons.wikimedia.org/wiki/File:Trombone_CG_Bach42
AG.jpg*

The tenor trombone is perhaps the most recognizable type, known for its versatile range and use in a wide range of musical genres, from classical to jazz and beyond.

Characteristics:

- **Slide Mechanism:** Like all trombones, the tenor trombone features a slide without valves, making pitch control reliant on the player's precise slide movements.

- **Range:** It spans low to high B, offering a broad tonal spectrum.

- **Versatility:** Its adaptability makes it an excellent choice for beginners and seasoned musicians.

The Bass Trombone: Deeper and Richer

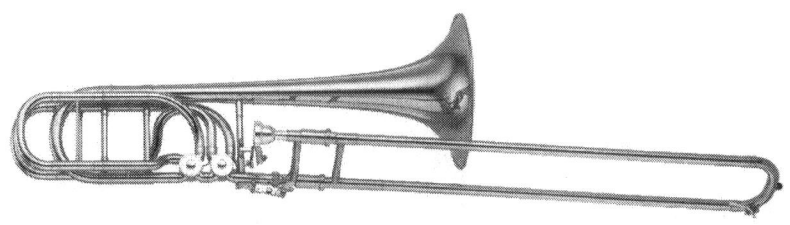

4.   *The base trombone can add a layer of richness to your music.*
Source: Yamaha Corporation, CC BY-SA 4.0
<https://creativecommons.org/licenses/by-sa/4.0>, via Wikimedia Commons:
https://commons.wikimedia.org/wiki/File:Yamaha_Bass_trombone_YBL-830_horizontal.tif

If you're looking for a trombone that dives deeper into the lower registers and adds a layer of richness to your music, the bass trombone is worth a look.

Characteristics:

- **Additional Valves:** The bass trombone often includes one or two valves, providing more control over pitch and extending the lower range.

- **Extended Tubing:** Longer tubing than the tenor trombone produces a lower pitch.

- **Versatile Sound:** It is ideal for playing lower parts in ensembles and adds depth and gravity to the music.

The Alto Trombone: A Baroque Beauty

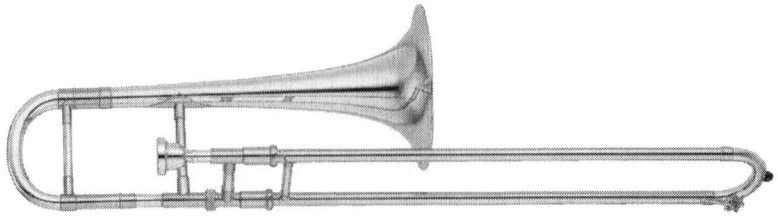

5. *The alto trombone has a higher-pitch than the tenor trombone.*
Source: Yamaha Corporation, CC BY-SA 4.0
<https://creativecommons.org/licenses/by-sa/4.0>, via Wikimedia
Commons:
https://commons.wikimedia.org/wiki/File:Yamaha_Alto_trombon
e_YSL-871.tif

The alto trombone is a smaller and higher-pitched cousin of the tenor trombone, known for its historical significance and use in baroque music.

Characteristics:

- **Higher Pitch:** It is smaller and brighter than the tenor trombone with a pitch in E or F.

- **Chamber Music:** Often chosen for chamber music and historically informed performances of baroque music.

- **Unique Sound:** Its distinctive timbre adds a touch of authenticity to period pieces.

The Valve Trombone: Simplified Precision

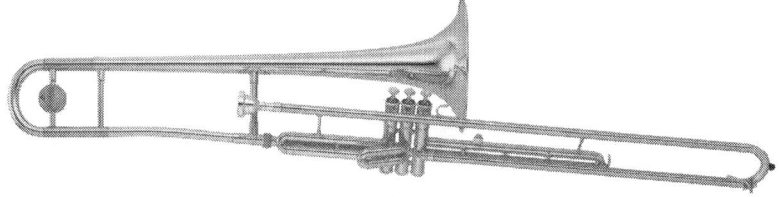

6. Valve trombones are easier for beginners. Source: Yamaha Corporation, CC BY-SA 4.0 <https://creativecommons.org/licenses/by-sa/4.0>, via Wikimedia Commons: https://commons.wikimedia.org/wiki/File:Yamaha_YSL-354_V_valve_trombone.png

As the name suggests, valve trombones incorporate valves into their design, making them easier to play for beginners and suitable for specific musical styles.

Characteristics:

- **Valves:** Valves allow players to change pitch without relying solely on slide movements.

- **Ease of Play:** Ideal for those new to the Trombone or for genres where rapid pitch changes are expected.

- **Dixieland Jazz:** Frequently used in Dixieland jazz due to its agility and responsiveness.

The Contrabass Trombone: Rare and Reverberant

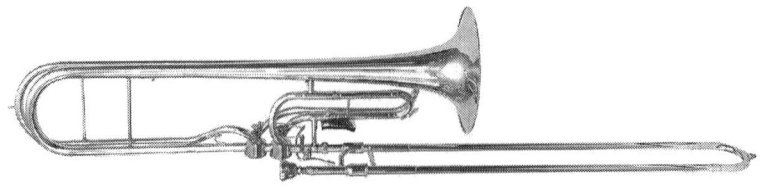

7. The contrabass trombone is the lowest-pitched member of the trombone family. Source: Jonathan Harker, CC BY 4.0 <https://creativecommons.org/licenses/by/4.0>, via Wikimedia Commons: https://commons.wikimedia.org/wiki/File:Wessex_contrabass_trombone_in_F.jpg

The contrabass trombone is the largest and lowest-pitched member of the trombone family, offering a truly unique and thunderous sound.

Characteristics:

- **Enormous Size:** It's massive, with a pitch extending to the depths of the bass clef.

- **Rareness:** Not commonly encountered, it's mainly used in specialized musical contexts and orchestral settings.

- **Orchestral Power:** When it appears, it adds a powerful and resonant bass foundation to the ensemble's sound.

Understanding the types of trombones allows musicians to make informed choices that align with their musical goals and preferences. Whether you're drawn to the tenor trombone's versatility or the bass trombone's richness, you must first decide on the type of music you will play before you select a trombone. Embrace the diversity of the trombone family, and let your choice reflect your musical expression and creativity.

Selecting the Right Mouthpiece and Accessories

The choice of mouthpiece and accessories significantly impacts your trombone-playing experience. While personal preferences come into play, it's essential to understand the different components and their effects on sound.

Choosing the Right Mouthpiece

8.   The mouthpiece bridges between you and your Trombone's sound. Source: Dhscommtech at English Wikipedia, CC BY-SA 3.0 <https://creativecommons.org/licenses/by-sa/3.0>, via Wikimedia Commons:

The mouthpiece is the bridge between you and your Trombone's sound. Here are some factors to consider when selecting the right one:

- **Cup Size:** Larger cups produce a darker sound, while smaller cups yield a brighter tone. Choose a cup size that aligns with your preferred style and musical genre.

- **Rim Shape:** The shape of the rim affects comfort and endurance. Experiment with different rim shapes to find one that suits your lips.

- **Throat Size:** A smaller throat size can enhance high notes, while a larger one may improve low notes. Balance this according to your playing needs.

- **Material:** Mouthpieces can be made of various materials, such as brass, stainless steel, or plastic. Each material imparts a distinct timbre to your sound.

Essential Accessories

In addition to your mouthpiece, there are essential accessories you should consider:

- **Trombone Case:** Invest in a sturdy case to protect your instrument from damage during transportation and storage.

- **Slide Lubricant:** Proper slide lubrication is essential for smooth sliding and tuning adjustments.

- **Cleaning Kit:** Keeping your Trombone clean is crucial for maintaining its performance. A cleaning kit will help you remove dirt and moisture.

- **Music Stand:** A stable music stand holds your sheet music at the right height and angle for comfortable playing.

- **Metronome:** A metronome improves your timing and rhythm.

- **Tuner:** A tuner helps you maintain accurate pitch, ensuring you play in tune.

By understanding the parts of your Trombone, exploring the different types available, and making informed choices regarding mouthpieces and accessories, you'll be well on your way to becoming a confident and capable trombonist. So, keep practicing, stay curious, and embrace the world of the Trombone with enthusiasm.

Chapter 3: The Basics of Trombone Playing

The Trombone is a unique and beautiful instrument, but it does require some initial guidance to get started on the right note (pun intended). This chapter focuses on the fundamental aspects that every aspiring trombonist, especially beginners, should grasp. You'll explore proper posture and body alignment to ensure comfort and prevent strain, and then learn the correct way to hold and move the trombone slide.

This chapter will also introduce you to the positions essential for producing different notes and provide an overview of trombone notation and terminology. By the end, you will have a solid foundation to build your trombone-playing skills.

Proper Posture and Body Alignment

Playing the Trombone is about producing beautiful music through proper posture and body alignment. Like any other musical instrument, good posture is essential for comfort, performance, and long-term well-being.

The Importance of Proper Posture

Proper posture and body alignment are the foundation of successful trombone playing. Here's why it matters:

- **Comfort and Endurance:** Playing the Trombone for an extended period can be physically demanding. Proper posture helps distribute the instrument's weight evenly across your body, reducing the risk of fatigue and discomfort.

- **Sound Quality:** Maintaining the correct posture ensures you have complete control over your breathing and embouchure (using your lips, tongue, and facial muscles to produce sound). This, in turn, directly affects the quality of sound you produce.

- **Injury Prevention:** Playing the Trombone with poor posture can lead to muscle strain, tension, and long-term injuries. Maintaining proper alignment will avoid unnecessary stress on your muscles and joints.

Tips for Proper Posture and Body Alignment

Now that we understand why good posture is essential, here are some practical tips to achieve it while playing the Trombone:

Stand Tall

- Start by standing with your feet shoulder-width apart. This provides a stable base.

- Keep your back straight and your shoulders relaxed. Avoid slouching, as this can restrict your lung capacity and affect your breathing.

- Imagine a string pulling you upward from the top of your head. This mental image can help you maintain an erect posture.

Position the Trombone Correctly

- Hold the Trombone with your left hand on the slide and your right hand on the bell section (or valve section, if applicable).

- The mouthpiece should align with your lips when you bring the Trombone to your mouth. This alignment ensures you're not straining your neck or contorting your body to reach the mouthpiece.

Align Your Head

- Keep your head in a neutral position, facing straight ahead. Avoid tilting it up or down, as this can strain your neck and affect your breathing.

- Your gaze should be directed at your music or conductor, not down at your Trombone.

Relax Your Arms

- Maintain relaxed arms. Your left arm should control the slide while your right arm supports the instrument's weight.

- Squeezing the Trombone too tightly can lead to tension and discomfort. A gentle, balanced grip is key.

Balance Your Weight

- Distribute your weight evenly between your legs. This balanced stance helps you stay stable while playing.

- Avoid shifting your weight to one side, which will lead to strain and discomfort.

Consider a Strap (Optional)

- Some trombonists find it helpful to use a shoulder strap or harness to support the instrument's weight. It alleviates strain on your arms and back.

- Experiment with different straps to find one that's comfortable for you.

Practicing Proper Posture

Achieving and maintaining proper posture while playing the Trombone may take time and conscious effort, especially for beginners. Here are some tips for practicing good posture:

- **Mirror Practice:** Use a mirror while practicing to check your posture. Visual feedback will help you make necessary adjustments.

- **Regular Breaks:** If you're playing for an extended period, take short breaks to stretch and reset your posture, preventing fatigue and discomfort.

- **Feedback from a Teacher:** If you're taking lessons, ask your teacher for feedback on your posture. They can provide valuable guidance and corrections.

- **Posture Exercises:** Incorporate posture exercises into your daily routine. These can help improve your overall posture while playing the Trombone and in everyday life.

Proper posture and body alignment are essential for trombone players of all levels. Whether a beginner or an experienced musician, maintaining good posture enhances your performance and ensures your long-term well-being. By following these tips and practicing consistently, you'll be well on your way to playing the Trombone easily and comfortably while producing beautiful music. So, stand tall, relax your shoulders, and let your Trombone sing with the grace of good posture.

Holding the Trombone and Sliding Correctly

9. *Holding your Trombone correctly will help you play it properly.*
Source: https://unsplash.com/photos/Ny-
KuNNhlgI?utm_source=unsplash&utm_medium=referral&utm_co
ntent=creditShareLink

Once you know how to stand, you can learn how to hold the Trombone and use the slide.

- **Left Hand on the Slide:** Your left hand controls the slide. Place your thumb on top of the slide, with your fingers gripping the bottom. Move the slide smoothly by extending and retracting your arm, not your wrist.

- **Right Hand on the Bell:** Your right hand supports the weight of the Trombone's bell or valve section. Hold it gently, allowing the instrument to pivot naturally as needed.

- **The Grip:** Maintain a relaxed grip with both hands. Squeezing the instrument too tightly can limit your ability to move the slide and create tension in your playing.

- **Slide Technique:** Use your forearm and upper arm muscles rather than your wrist when moving the slide. Ensure that the slide moves smoothly and evenly. A well-maintained slide will facilitate this.

Introduction to the Positions and Slide Movements

Understanding the positions and slide movements is the core of playing the Trombone. These positions determine the notes you produce, so mastering them is essential.

1. **First Position:** This is the starting point. With the slide fully retracted, you play the fundamental B♭. The first position is often marked with a Roman numeral "I" in music notation.

2. **Second Position:** Extend the slide to the second position to produce a B. The "II" in the notation indicates the second position.

3. **Third Position:** Move to the third position ("III") for a G.

4. **Fourth Position:** Slide to the fourth position ("IV") to achieve F.

5. **Fifth Position:** This position results in an E. You'll see "V" in your music to indicate the fifth position.

6. **Sixth Position:** Extend the slide to the sixth position for an open note, often marked as "VI" or "O" in notation.

7. **Seventh Position:** This position yields a D, denoted by "VII" in sheet music.

8. **Eighth Position:** The eighth position, marked as "VIII," produces a C.

To create the notes between these positions, you must develop your muscle memory and learn to accurately gauge the distances between each position. Regular practice is key to mastering this aspect of trombone playing.

Overview of Trombone Notation and Terminology

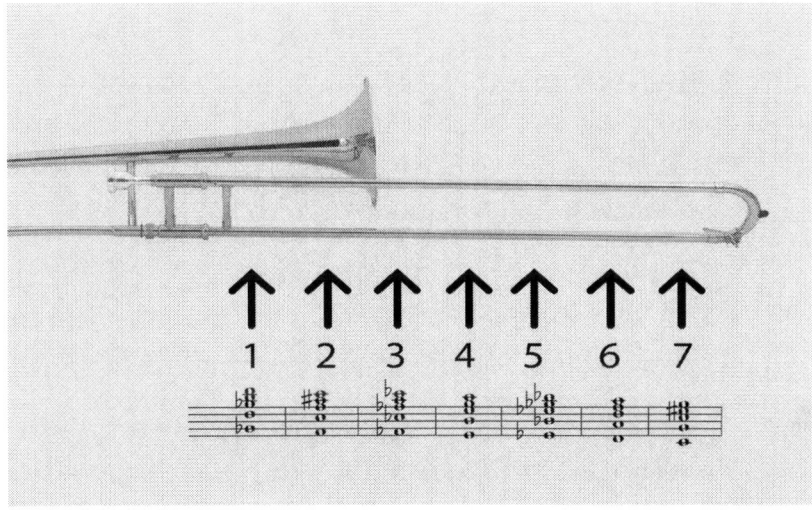

10. *Understanding the notations and terminology related to trombones is important for effective interpretation of music. Source: https://www.digitaltrombone.com/wp-content/uploads/2012/03/Trombone-slide-chart-featured.png*

As with any musical instrument, understanding the notation and terminology specific to the Trombone is crucial for effective communication and interpretation of music.

- **Treble Clef:** Trombone music is typically notated in the treble clef, also known as the G clef. This clef tells you which notes correspond to the lines and spaces on the staff.

- **Positions and Note Names:** Familiarize yourself with the positions and their corresponding note names. This knowledge is essential for reading and playing music accurately.

- **Dynamics:** Dynamics refers to the loudness or softness of the music. Common dynamic markings include "piano" (soft), "forte" (loud), and various gradations in between.

- **Articulation:** Articulation markings instruct you on how to attack and release each note. Common articulations include "legato" (smooth and connected) and "staccato" (short and detached).

- **Tempo Markings:** Tempo markings indicate the speed at which a piece should be played. Familiar terms include "allegro" (fast), "adagio" (slow), and "andante" (moderate).

- **Key Signature:** Pay attention to the key signature at the beginning of a piece. It tells you which notes are sharp or flat throughout the music.

- **Time Signature:** Time signatures like 4/4 or 3/4 indicate the number of beats per measure and the type of note that receives one beat.

- **Rests:** Rests signify periods of silence in the music. Different types of rests (whole, half, quarter, etc.) indicate varying durations of silence.

With a grasp of these basic elements of notation and terminology, you'll be better equipped to read and interpret trombone music effectively.

As you embark on your trombone-playing journey, remember that mastering these fundamentals takes time and practice. Be patient with yourself, and remember that even the most skilled trombonists started with the basics. With dedication and a commitment to learning, you'll gradually build the skills and knowledge necessary to play this beautiful instrument confidently and skillfully. So, keep practicing, stay curious, and let the music guide your trombone adventure.

Chapter 4: Proper Embouchure and Breath Control

Playing a musical instrument is an enriching experience but requires patience and dedication. One of the fundamental aspects of mastering any wind instrument, whether the flute, clarinet, saxophone, or trumpet, is understanding your embouchure and breath control and perfecting your techniques. In this chapter, you'll dive into the essential techniques and concepts that will help you produce a beautiful and consistent tone.

Understanding the Importance of Embouchure in Tone Production

11. Embouchure is crucial to achieving a great sound. Source: https://unsplash.com/photos/qrb_gnikcl8?utm_source=unsplash& utm_medium=referral&utm_content=creditShareLink

Before you delve into the techniques for forming a proper embouchure, you must first grasp why it's crucial to achieving a great sound. Your embouchure is how you shape and control your mouth and facial muscles when playing a wind instrument. It's the bridge between your breath and the instrument. It influences the quality, pitch, and articulation of the sound produced.

The Role of Embouchure

The embouchure determines how your airstream interacts with the instrument's mouthpiece or reed. A well-formed embouchure can:

- **Control Pitch:** By adjusting the tension and position of your lips and facial muscles, you can fine-tune the pitch of each note you play.

- **Shape Tone:** Your embouchure creates a rich and resonant sound. You're the sculptor shaping a piece of clay, molding the sound to your liking.

- **Articulate Notes:** How you shape your embouchure impacts how crisply or smoothly you articulate notes, enhancing the expressiveness of your music.

Techniques for Forming a Proper Embouchure

While the specifics may vary depending on your instrument, the basic principles remain relatively consistent.

Lip Positioning

- **Begin with a Relaxed Smile:** Your lips should be relaxed but not slack. Imagine you're smiling gently, which will help you find the right balance.

- **Tuck the Corners in Slightly:** The corners of your mouth should be drawn in just a bit, creating a subtle "U" shape, providing stability and control.

- **Place Your Top Teeth on the Mouthpiece:** For many brass and woodwind instruments, lightly rest your top teeth on the mouthpiece or reed. This serves as a reference point for consistent positioning.

Lip Pressure

- **Balanced Pressure:** Apply just enough pressure to create an airtight seal without straining your facial muscles. Finding the right balance may take some time and experimentation.

- **Stay Flexible:** Adjust your embouchure as needed when transitioning between registers or articulations.

Tongue Position

- **Keep Your Tongue Relaxed:** Your tongue should rest gently on the floor of your mouth. Avoid pressing it too firmly against the reed or mouthpiece, as this can stifle airflow and affect tone quality.

- **Vary Your Tongue Placement:** Depending on the register you're playing, you may need to adjust the height and placement of your tongue. Experiment to find what works best.

Jaw Placement

- **Open Your Jaw Slightly:** Depending on your instrument, you may need to open your jaw a little to allow proper airflow. Consult your teacher or refer to instrument-specific resources for guidance.

- **Be Mindful of Your Jaw Position:** Keep your jaw relaxed and in the same position throughout a passage. Unwanted shifting can throw off intonation, articulation, and tone quality.

Experiment and Adapt

- **Embrace Experimentation:** Finding the perfect embouchure may require some trial and error. Be patient and open to adjusting your technique as you progress.

- **Listen for Sound Clarity:** A great embouchure produces a rich, consistent tone and ensures that each note is clear and complete. Listen carefully as you play, and adjust your form accordingly.

As you refine your embouchure, you'll also focus on developing proper breath control. While breathing correctly is essential for all instruments, it's especially crucial when playing a wind instrument. By honing your breathing technique, you will create a consistent and powerful air stream that propels the sound of your music.

Developing Breath Control and Managing Airflow for Consistent Sound

Breath control is the engine that drives your instrument, and understanding how to harness it is essential for consistent and expressive sound production. The better your breathing technique, the more you can control the dynamic range and tonal quality of your playing.

The Importance of Breath Control

Your breath is the fuel that powers your musical journey. Without proper control and management, your instrument won't respond as needed, and your tone will suffer. Here's why breath control is indispensable:

- **Sustain Notes:** Effective breath control enables you to hold notes for extended periods, allowing you to create beautiful, sustained melodies.

- **Dynamic Expression:** You can vary the volume and intensity of your playing by adjusting your breath support, allowing for dynamic and emotionally charged performances.

- **Articulation:** Controlling your airflow precisely lets you articulate notes crisply or smoothly, adding nuance to your music.

Techniques for Developing Breath Control

Mastering breath control is gradual, but you can make significant improvements with practice and dedication. Here are five techniques to help you along the way:

1. **Diaphragmatic Breathing:** When you inhale, focus on expanding your diaphragm rather than raising your shoulders. This deepens your breath and provides better control. Take slow, full breaths and observe how your abdomen rises as you do so. Eventually, this will become more natural.

2. **Consistent Pressure:** Aim for a consistent stream of air when playing. Avoid sudden bursts or declines in pressure, as these can disrupt your tone. Instead, focus on sustaining a steady flow of air throughout each note.

3. **Engage Your Core Muscles:** To sustain long notes or play at louder volumes, engage your core muscles to provide steady support for your breath. The key is to develop the right balance between your core and breathing muscles.

4. **Practice with a Metronome:** Use a metronome to practice sustaining notes for longer durations. Gradually increase the length of your notes to build endurance. To further challenge yourself, practice playing multiple notes on a single breath.

5. **Vary Your Breath Intensity:** Practice playing the same passage at different dynamic levels by adjusting

your breath support. This helps you understand how airflow impacts tone. For example, a louder passage will require more breath support than a softer one.

Developing proper embouchure and breath control is an ongoing process. Consistent practice, feedback from a teacher, and patience are your allies on this musical journey. As you work on these foundational elements, your tone becomes more expressive and your music more captivating.

Practical Exercises: A Deeper Dive

Long Tones

Long tones are the foundation of developing a beautiful, sustained sound on the Trombone. To practice this exercise effectively, follow these steps:

1. Choose a comfortable note within your range.

2. Begin playing the note at a mezzo-forte (moderate volume) dynamic level.

3. Sustain the note for as long as possible, aiming for a smooth and consistent tone.

4. As you progress, challenge yourself to play the note at different dynamic levels, from pianissimo (very soft) to fortissimo (very loud).

5. Pay close attention to your breath control and embouchure to maintain a steady sound.

Long tones are an excellent way to develop your tone quality. They build endurance and refine your sense of pitch.

Lip Slurs

Lip slurs are a fantastic exercise for enhancing your embouchure strength and control, essential for managing airflow and articulation. Here's how to practice lip slurs effectively:

1. Start with a comfortable note in the middle of your range.

2. Play this note without using the slide, smoothly and gradually changing to a higher or lower note.

3. The goal is to achieve a seamless transition between the notes without any discernible "bumps" or changes in tone quality.

4. Gradually increase the range of your lip slurs as your embouchure strength improves.

5. Experiment with different patterns and intervals to challenge yourself.

Lip slurs improve your embouchure and ability to control the airspeed and direction within the mouthpiece, which is crucial for consistent sound production.

Metronome Practice

Using a metronome to develop steady airflow is a valuable technique that enhances your sense of timing and rhythm. Here's how to make the most of metronome practice:

1. Set the metronome to a comfortable tempo.

2. Play a simple scale or long-tone exercise, aligning your breaths with the metronome's beat.

3. As you become more comfortable, increase the metronome's tempo to challenge yourself.

This exercise helps you synchronize your breath control with the tempo of the music, ensuring a consistent and steady sound. Metronome practice improves your timing and trains you to maintain a steady airflow even when playing complex passages with varying rhythms.

Breathing Gymnastics

Breathing exercises, often called "breathing gymnastics," are vital for expanding your lung capacity and developing precise breath control. Here are a few exercises to try:

- **Breath Holds:** Inhale deeply and hold your breath for as long as possible. Gradually extend the duration of your breath holds. This exercise increases your lung capacity and strengthens your respiratory muscles.

- **Quick Inhalations:** Practice taking quick, controlled inhalations, almost like "sniffs" of air. This exercise trains your body to efficiently replenish your air supply during rests in the music, ensuring you have enough air for sustained playing.

- **Sustained Exhalations:** Inhale deeply and then exhale slowly and steadily for as long as possible. This exercise helps you develop control over your exhalation rate, which is crucial for phrases with varying dynamics and lengths.

- **Breath Control with Scales:** Play scales while focusing on controlled and even breaths between each note. This exercise helps you apply breath control directly to your music.

These breathing exercises build endurance, maximize your breath capacity, and fine-tune your ability to manage airflow.

Incorporating these practical exercises into your daily routine will elevate your Trombone playing. Consistency and patience are key to mastering breath control and airflow management. Over time, you'll notice a significant improvement in the consistency and beauty of your sound on the Trombone.

With the right combination of embouchure and breath control, you can access a wealth of musical possibilities. As you become more familiar with your instrument, refine these essential elements and explore what they can do for your sound. With dedication and practice, you'll turn any musical passage into a masterpiece.

Chapter 5: Producing Your First Notes

Producing your first notes on a trombone opens the door to a world of musical expression. The Trombone, with its rich history and unique sliding mechanism, offers a distinctive voice in brass instruments. You'll need patience, dedication, and a fundamental understanding of the instrument on this musical journey.

It's time to dive right in and start producing your first notes. This chapter is all about practicality. It'll guide you through getting sound out of your Trombone and achieving pitch accuracy.

Getting Started: Fundamental Notes and Pitch Accuracy

Before you play full melodies, start with the basics of producing fundamental notes and honing your pitch accuracy. Think of these initial steps as building blocks upon which you'll construct your musical skills.

12. Understanding fundamental notes will help you master the Trombone. Source: https://unsplash.com/photos/2Q9L3UwjWz8

Understanding Fundamental Notes

Fundamental notes are the foundation of any musical piece. On the Trombone, these notes are generated by adjusting the position of the slide. To produce your first notes:

1. **Position Your Body:** Establish the proper physical foundation. Whether you stand or sit, ensure your body posture is upright and relaxed. This provides the ideal platform for sound production.

2. **Embouchurc Formation:** Next, focus on your embouchure, the intricate interplay of your lips and facial muscles at the heart of brass instrument playing. Place your lips firmly against the mouthpiece, creating an airtight seal. Picture yourself forming the letter 'M' with your lips.

3. **Buzzing:** Before you move on to the Trombone itself, acquaint yourself with the art of buzzing. Buzzing involves vibrating your lips while maintaining the embouchure shape you've just perfected. It's somewhat akin to making a 'raspberry' sound. Experiment with different levels of lip tension to discover the optimal buzz for each note.

4. **Slide Position:** The Trombone's unique sound production relies heavily on the slide. It allows you to change the instrument's length and pitch. As a beginner, focus on the note Bb (concert C). Locate the correct slide position to produce this note.

5. **Combine Buzzing and Slide:** Now comes the exciting part. While buzzing your lips, carefully move the slide to produce the Bb note. It may take a few attempts to nail the pitch precisely, so don't be discouraged. Learning to control the slide is a skill that develops with practice.

6. **Listening for Pitch:** Pay close attention to the pitch of your note. It's crucial to train your ear early on. Use a tuner or a keyboard to verify you are hitting the correct pitch. Precision in pitch is a fundamental aspect of playing the Trombone.

7. **Practice Regularly:** Consistency is vital when it comes to producing fundamental notes. Dedicate time daily to refining your embouchure, slide positions, and pitch accuracy. The more you practice, the more comfortable and precise your note production will become.

Pitch Accuracy Tips

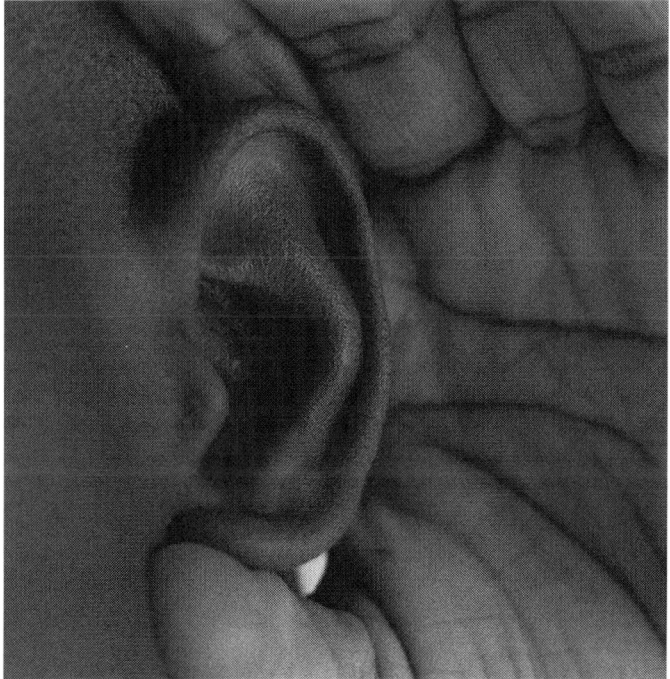

13. Ear training can help your pitch become more accurate. Source: https://unsplash.com/photos/oxaBYAbpWgI?utm_source=unsplas h&utm_medium=referral&utm_content=creditShareLink

To further enhance your pitch accuracy, consider these tips:

- **Ear Training:** Immerse yourself in the sounds of professional trombonists. Listen to a wide range of music and play along with recordings. This exposes you to different musical styles and helps you internalize the correct pitch.

- **Tuner Usage:** A reliable tuner is a trombonist's best friend. Invest in a good-quality tuner and make tuning your instrument a regular routine. Additionally, use the tuner during practice sessions to fine-tune your pitch accuracy.

- **Long Tones:** The magic of long tones lies in their simplicity. You develop control and pitch stability by holding a single note for an extended period. Start with fundamental notes and gradually extend the duration as you progress.

- **Dynamic Playing:** Experiment with dynamic playing by varying the intensity of your notes. This adds depth to your sound and helps you explore different pitches and tone qualities.

Producing notes on a trombone requires practice and dedication. By mastering the fundamentals of pitch production, you'll be on your way to playing beautiful music. Don't forget to enjoy the journey. Have fun and don't get discouraged if progress is slow. With patience and consistency, anyone can become a trombonist.

Buzzing and Mouthpiece Exercises for Tone Improvement

Now that you've laid the foundation with fundamental notes and pitch accuracy, it's time to turn your attention to tone improvement. Achieving a rich and resonant tone is a hallmark of an accomplished trombonist. Buzzing and mouthpiece exercises are powerful tools in your journey to achieve this musical milestone.

Buzzing Exercises

Buzzing exercises revolve around producing notes using only the mouthpiece. Here's how to develop this aspect of tone development:

1. **Warm-Up:** Begin each practice session with lip buzzing to warm up your embouchure. Without the mouthpiece, buzz your lips to create a consistent, even sound. This simple exercise prepares your lips and facial muscles for more demanding work.

2. **Descending Buzzing:** Progress to buzzing a series of descending notes, starting from a comfortable pitch and moving downward chromatically. Concentrate on maintaining a clear, resonant buzz throughout the descent.

3. **Ascending Buzzing:** Practice ascending notes using the same approach. Ascending buzzing helps you gain control over your embouchure and further refines your tone.

4. **Buzzing Scales:** Now, apply your buzzing skills to scales. Work on major and minor scales, and practice moving up and down the tonal spectrum. This exercise improves your tone and enhances your familiarity with different scales.

Mouthpiece Exercises

Mouthpiece exercises introduce additional challenges for your embouchure and tone development.

- **Long Tones:** Long tones on the mouthpiece are akin to a meditative practice for trombonists. By sustaining a single note for an extended duration, you build endurance and cultivate a steady, resonant sound.

Focus on maintaining consistent tone quality throughout each note's duration.

- **Articulation:** Precision in articulation is a hallmark of advanced trombonists. On the mouthpiece, practice articulating notes clearly and crisply. This exercise enhances your control and precision, allowing you to articulate musical passages clearly and confidently.

- **Scales and Arpeggios:** Challenge yourself by working on scales and arpeggios using just the mouthpiece. This exercise sharpens your ability to navigate different musical patterns, setting the stage for more complex melodies.

- **Interval Jumps:** Expand your tonal range and strengthen your embouchure by practicing interval jumps. With precision and control, leap between intervals, such as octaves or fifths. This exercise builds technical proficiency and adds depth to your tonal palette.

These exercises are a great starting point for beginners. As you progress, incorporate new concepts into your practice routine to refine your tone and embouchure control. With consistent practice and dedication, you'll soon be playing the Trombone with beautiful resonance and clarity.

Transitioning from Buzzing to Playing on the Trombone

With firmly established buzzing and mouthpiece exercises, you're now prepared to transition to playing on the Trombone. This is a momentous step in your trombone journey, as you'll apply the skills you've honed directly to your instrument.

Mouthpiece to Trombone

1. **Prepare Your Trombone:** Before you begin, ensure your Trombone is well-maintained and lubricated. A clean and functioning instrument is essential for optimal sound production.

2. **Choose a Comfortable Note:** As you move from mouthpiece to Trombone, start with the same Bb note you've been practicing. Position your slide to match the desired note.

3. **Embouchure Transition:** Transfer the embouchure you've perfected during buzzing exercises to the Trombone's mouthpiece. This transition should be smooth, allowing you to maintain embouchure integrity.

4. **Gentle Start:** Begin by gently blowing air through the Trombone while maintaining your buzzing embouchure. At this stage, the goal isn't to produce full, resonant notes but to initiate sound production on the instrument.

5. **Slide Control:** Pay special attention to controlling the slide's movement as you play. This is a skill that will significantly impact your pitch accuracy. Practice moving the slide smoothly and precisely to match the desired notes.

6. **Experiment and Explore:** Once you feel comfortable, explore different trombone notes and scales. Apply the techniques you've developed through buzzing and mouthpiece exercises to your playing.

With diligent practice, you'll build muscle memory and refine your tone on the instrument.

Transitioning from buzzing to playing on the Trombone will require patience. It's normal to encounter challenges as you adapt to the new dynamics of the instrument. Celebrate each small victory, and don't forget to record your practice sessions. Listening to your playing will provide valuable insights into your tone, pitch accuracy, and overall progress.

Producing your first notes on the Trombone is a rewarding and essential step in your musical journey. Start with fundamental notes and pitch accuracy, practice buzzing and mouthpiece exercises to refine your tone, and gradually transition to playing on the Trombone. With dedication and consistent practice, you'll soon create beautiful melodies on this magnificent instrument. Keep up the great work, and remember that every note you play brings you closer to becoming a skilled trombonist.

Chapter 6: Learning Basic Techniques

In music, the Trombone stands out as a truly unique instrument. Its rich, resonant tones and striking visual presence have captured the hearts of many musicians and music enthusiasts alike. But to truly harness the magic of this brass beauty, you must learn and master its basic techniques.

Exploring Different Articulation Techniques

Articulation is how you shape and define your musical phrases. It allows you to create nuanced sounds that other instruments cannot achieve. Here are five fundamental articulation techniques to help you express yourself clearly and emotionally.

Legato: The Smooth Operator

14. *Legato music notation. Source: File:Music-legato.png:
Denelson83Vectorisation: Ekips39, CC BY-SA 3.0
<http://creativecommons.org/licenses/by-sa/3.0/>, via Wikimedia
Commons: https://commons.wikimedia.org/wiki/File:Music-
legato.svg*

Legato, derived from the Italian word for "tied together," is a technique that emphasizes seamless, smooth transitions between notes. It's a gentle, flowing river of sound. To achieve legato on the Trombone, follow these steps:

1. **Use Your Air Support:** Your breath is the engine that powers your sound. Maintain a steady, controlled flow of air to create fluid connections between notes. Without strong and consistent airflow, your legato will lack the desired fluidity.

2. **Minimal Tongue Action:** Legato relies on minimal tongue movement. Think of your tongue as a feather, lightly caressing the notes. Avoid using excessive

tongue pressure, as it can disrupt the smoothness of your phrases.

3. **Slide Control:** Pay close attention to your slide movements. Gradual, precise slides are key to achieving that connected, legato sound. Practice moving the slide smoothly between notes without any sudden jerks or hesitations. The slide should complement the airflow to create a seamless legato effect.

Staccato: The Quick and Crisp

15. Staccato is the opposite of legato. Source: Radivoj Lazić (Radivojl), CC BY-SA 3.0 <https://creativecommons.org/licenses/by-sa/3.0>, via Wikimedia Commons: https://commons.wikimedia.org/wiki/File:Staccato_izvedba.jpg

Staccato is the polar opposite of legato. It's all about short, detached notes that excite and contrast your music. To master staccato on the Trombone, follow these steps:

1. **Tongue Articulation:** Your tongue becomes your ally here. Quick, precise tonguing is crucial to creating those crisp, separated sounds—practice using the tip of your tongue to start and stop the airflow rapidly for each note.

2. **Percussive Air:** Use short bursts of air to give your notes that punchy, staccato feel. Think of it like playing a musical drumbeat. This quick release of air sets staccato apart from legato's sustained airflow.

3. **Slide Control:** Be deliberate in your slide positions to ensure each note is distinct. It may require faster slide movements than legato, but precision remains crucial.

Marcato: The Emphatic Articulation

16. *Marcato emphasizes music notes. Source: Hyacinth, Public domain, via Wikimedia Commons: https://commons.wikimedia.org/wiki/File:Diatonic_scale_on_C_marcato.png*

Marcato is about making a bold statement. It's similar to underlining a word for emphasis in a sentence. To achieve marcato on the Trombone:

1. **Strong Tonguing:** Unlike the light tonguing of legato, marcato demands forceful and deliberate tonguing. Use the tip of your tongue with authority to start each note.

2. **Powerful Air Support:** Your airflow should match the strength of your tonguing. Project your sound to the back of the room. This combination of forceful tongue and air creates the powerful marcato effect.

3. **Accentuated Slide Movements:** Emphasize the slide movements to make each note stand out. While not as detached as staccato, marcato requires clearly defined note beginnings and endings.

Tenuto: The Sustained Embrace

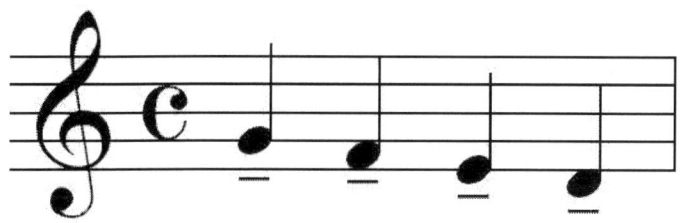

17. Tenuto is about holding onto the full value of each note. Source: Radivoj Lazić (Radivojl), CC BY-SA 3.0 <https://creativecommons.org/licenses/by-sa/3.0>, via Wikimedia Commons: https://commons.wikimedia.org/wiki/File:Tenuto.jpg

Tenuto gives each note a loving embrace. It's about holding onto the full value of each note and making it sing. To achieve tenuto on the trombone:

1. **Controlled Tonguing:** While not as forceful as marcato, tenuto still requires precise tonguing. Give each note a gentle nudge to ensure it plays for its full duration.

2. **Steady Airflow:** Maintain a steady stream of air to sustain each note. Consistency is key here. Sculpt the note's shape with your breath.

3. **Slide Control:** Unlike staccato or marcato, your slide control is more subtle in tenuto. It should support the note's entire duration without drawing attention away from its beauty.

Sforzando (Sforzato): The Dramatic Accent

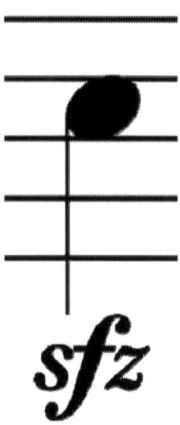

18. Sforzando is a way of adding a dramatic flair to a note. Source: Wimopul, CC BY-SA 4.0 <https://creativecommons.org/licenses/by-sa/4.0>, via Wikimedia Commons: https://commons.wikimedia.org/wiki/File:Sfz_own_world.png

Sforzando, often abbreviated as "sfz" or "sf," is the Trombone's way of adding a dramatic flair to a note. It's like shouting a word in the middle of a sentence to grab attention. To achieve sforzando on the trombone:

1. **Sudden Intensity:** Start the note with a sudden burst of intensity, both in tonguing and airflow. It's a musical exclamation mark.

2. **Immediate Release:** After the initial burst of intensity, immediately ease off while maintaining the note's volume. It creates the dramatic accent characteristic of sforzando.

3. **Slide as an Accent:** The slide can also play a role in accentuating the sforzando. A slight slide movement can emphasize the note's intensity, but be careful not to overdo it.

These five articulation techniques offer many expressive possibilities on the Trombone. Mastering these techniques will allow you to convey your musical ideas with precision and emotion, making your Trombone playing truly captivating.

Introduction to Vibrato and Other Expressive Techniques

In the world of music, it's not just about playing the right notes. It's also about how you play them. Trombonists have a rich palette of expressive techniques at their disposal. The following techniques will elevate your Trombone playing to a new level of expressiveness.

Vibrato: Adding Warmth and Emotion

Vibrato is a gentle shimmer in your sound, adding warmth and emotion to your Trombone playing. It's a technique that creates subtle variations in pitch, giving your notes a living, breathing quality. Vibrato is a powerful tool for conveying feelings in your music.

How to Achieve Vibrato:

1. **Finger Vibrato:** Start by practicing vibrato with your left hand. Gently roll your finger back and forth on the slide while maintaining a steady airflow. This subtle movement will introduce vibrato into your sound.

2. **Jaw Vibrato:** For a more pronounced vibrato, experiment with jaw movement. Keep your embouchure stable and allow your jaw to create pitch variations.

3. **Control is Key:** Vibrato should be a controlled, intentional technique. Practice varying the speed and depth of your vibrato to convey different emotions in your music.

Remember, vibrato is a seasoning, so use it sparingly to enhance the musical message you want to convey.

Mutes: Shaping Your Sound

Mutes are accessories that alter the tonal qualities of your Trombone. They are placed in the instrument's bell to produce various effects, from mellow and subdued to bright and edgy.

- **Straight Mute:** This mute produces a bright, focused sound with a metallic edge. It's often used for jazz and can add a distinctive flavor to your Trombone playing.

- **Cup Mute:** The cup mute creates a warmer, more muffled sound. It's excellent for creating a smoky, sultry atmosphere.

- **Plunger Mute:** A simple household plunger can be used as a mute! It creates a vocal, wah-wah effect and is often used in traditional jazz.

- **Bucket Mute:** This mute gives your Trombone a hollow, almost eerie quality. It's great for creating unique textures in your music.

Experiment with different mutes to discover the tonal possibilities they offer. Mutes add character and depth to your Trombone playing, making your sound distinctive.

Trills: Adding Sparkle and Flair

Trills are rapid alternations between two adjacent notes. They add a touch of sparkle and flair to your music, creating excitement and interest. Here's how to master trills:

1. **Finger Control:** Trills require nimble finger control. Practice trilling between two notes, gradually increasing your speed and precision.

2. **Use a Metronome:** A metronome helps you maintain an even trill speed. Start slow and gradually increase the tempo as you become more comfortable.

3. **Incorporate Trills Sparingly:** Trills are best used as embellishments, not as the main event. Use them strategically to highlight specific moments in your music.

Flutter Tongue: The Whimsical Effect

Flutter tongue is a quirky, whimsical technique that adds a unique texture to your Trombone playing. It involves rolling your "R" sound while playing to create a fluttering effect. Here's how to do it:

1. **Tongue Placement:** Position your tongue on the roof of your mouth, similar to the "R" sound in some languages.

2. **Gentle Pressure:** As you blow air through the Trombone, create gentle pressure with your tongue to make it flutter.

3. **Practice Control:** Flutter tongue can be wild and unpredictable at first. Practice controlling the speed and intensity of the flutter for different effects.

Flutter tongue is often used for playful or comedic musical moments, so have fun experimenting with it.

Incorporating these expressive trombone techniques into your playing will make you a more versatile trombonist. They'll add depth and emotion to your music. Whether you're gently applying vibrato for a soulful ballad or using a plunger mute for a jazzy improvisation, these techniques all add levels of richness and creativity.

Developing Smooth and Fluid Slide Movements

The Trombone's signature feature is, of course, its slide. This unique design allows you to play a continuous range of notes. However, it requires precise control for smooth transitions. Here's how to master the slide:

- **Finger Positioning:** Your left hand is your slide's guide. Position your fingers on the slide brace, ensuring a secure grip. The grip should be firm but not overly tight, allowing easy slide movement.

- **Practice Scales:** Start with simple scales to get comfortable with slide movements. Pay attention to the positions of the slide for each note and work on smooth transitions. As you ascend and descend the scale, focus on maintaining a consistent pitch and avoiding abrupt jumps.

- **Use Your Ears:** Listen for the pitch of each note as you slide. Your ears are your best feedback mechanism for slide control. Developing a keen ear for intonation is essential for becoming a skilled trombonist. If a note sounds out of tune, adjust your slide position accordingly.

- **Slow and Steady:** Speed will come with time, but initially, focus on slow, controlled slide movements. Precision trumps speed when it comes to mastering the slide. Smooth and deliberate slide transitions are key to playing accurately and expressively.

Exercises to Improve Finger Dexterity and Slide Coordination

Becoming proficient on the Trombone requires strong embouchure and breath control, nimble fingers, and coordinated slide movements.

Finger Dexterity Exercises

- **Scale Patterns:** Play scales in different keys, emphasizing finger agility. Challenge yourself with third, fourth, and fifth scales to promote flexibility. Scales are the foundation of your finger technique, and mastering them in various patterns will improve your overall dexterity.

- **Arpeggios:** Practice arpeggio patterns to improve finger independence. Start with basic triads and gradually move to more complex arpeggios. Arpeggios enhance your finger dexterity and help you navigate different tonalities in your music.

- **Chromatic Runs:** Play chromatic scales, focusing on accurate finger placement and smooth transitions. This exercise helps with slide coordination as well. Chromatic runs are beneficial for developing precise finger control and building muscle memory.

Slide Coordination Exercises

- **Glissandos:** Slide smoothly between two notes without tonguing. This exercise trains your slide control and ear for pitch. Start with simple intervals and progress to more challenging ones. Glissandos are a fun way to explore the full range of your instrument.

- **Interval Leaps:** Practice jumping between notes of varying intervals using the slide. Start with small intervals and work your way up to more significant jumps. Interval leaps will improve your slide accuracy and enhance your ability to navigate complex passages.

- **Long Tones with Slides:** Play sustained notes while gradually moving the slide to different positions. This exercise enhances your slide precision. Long tones with slides are excellent for developing a sense of control and intonation while moving the slide.

Progress on the Trombone is gradual, so be patient with yourself. Regular and focused practice on these basic techniques and exercises will set a strong foundation for your trombone journey.

The Trombone is a captivating instrument that rewards dedication and practice. By exploring articulation techniques, diving into expressive elements like vibrato, mastering slide control, and diligently working on finger dexterity and slide coordination, you'll unlock the full potential of this brass marvel. Embrace the learning process, and soon you'll be making music that resonates with your audience.

Chapter 7: Playing Simple Melodies

Welcome to the heart of your trombone journey! You've already taken your first steps, mastering fundamental notes, pitch accuracy, and tone production. It's time to bring the music to life by playing simple melodies.

This chapter is an exciting milestone in your musical adventure. You'll explore techniques tailored for beginner-friendly melodies and decode the mysteries of basic sheet music for the Trombone. You'll also dive into the world of rhythm and musical phrasing. By the end of this chapter, you'll be playing your favorite tunes confidently.

Applying Techniques to Play Beginner-Friendly Melodies

19. Playing beginner-friendly melodies can help you play harder compositions. Source: https://pixabay.com/photos/music-book-music-sheet-musical-notes-6168179/

Before you start playing full-fledged compositions, you must grasp the techniques to play beginner-friendly melodies. These melodies serve as stepping stones in your musical journey, allowing you to apply the skills you've acquired in a more musical context.

Breath Control and Dynamics

Breath control is the cornerstone of playing melodies. Your breath directly influences the Trombone's sound. Here's how to get started:

- **Deep Breathing:** Begin by practicing deep breaths. Inhale slowly through your nose, allowing your diaphragm to expand fully and providing a reservoir of air to sustain your notes.

- **Controlled Exhalation:** As you play, exhale steadily and consistently. Avoid the temptation to release all your air at once. Instead, aim for controlled, continuous airflow.

- **Dynamic Range:** Experiment with dynamics by varying the intensity of your breath. Practice playing both louder and softer to develop a wide dynamic range, adding expressiveness to your melodies.

- **Legato and Staccato:** Explore legato (smooth and connected) and staccato (short and detached) articulations. These techniques influence the character of your melodies. Legato creates flowing, lyrical lines, while staccato adds a crisp, punctuated quality.

Lip Slurs and Articulation

Lip slurs and articulation techniques are essential for navigating melodies with precision and clarity.

- **Lip Slurs:** Lip slurs involve smoothly moving between different notes without using the slide. Start with simple two-note slurs and gradually progress to more complex patterns. Lip slur exercises improve your embouchure control and note transitions.

- **Articulation:** Articulation refers to how you start and stop each note. Experiment with various articulation patterns, such as tonguing the beginning of each note for a crisp attack or using a legato tongue for smoother transitions. Articulation dramatically influences the character of your melodies.

- **Sustain and Vibrato:** Work on sustaining notes and experimenting with vibrato. Sustaining notes allow for expressive phrasing, while vibrato adds warmth and depth to your sound.

Reading and Interpreting Basic Sheet Music for the Trombone

Understanding sheet music is an essential skill for any musician. As a trombonist, it's a skill you'll rely on regularly. The basics of reading music for the Trombone are not as daunting as they may seem. The following sheet music elements will help you decipher and translate the musical code into beautiful trombone melodies.

The Staff and Clef

The staff is the very foundation of written music. It consists of a set of horizontal lines and spaces where musical symbols are placed. For the Trombone, you will primarily read music written in the bass clef, also known as the F clef. The bass clef symbol resembles an intricate backward 'S' with two dots. It indicates that the notes you'll read on the staff correspond to lower pitches. The Trombone's tonal range aligns perfectly with the bass clef, making it the standard choice for trombonists.

Each line and space on the staff represents a different pitch. Starting from the bottom line and moving upward, the lines and spaces correspond to specific notes:

- The lines, from bottom to top, represent the notes G, B, D, F, and A. Remember this mnemonic: "Good Boys Deserve Fudge Always."

- The spaces from bottom to top represent the notes F, A, C, and E. To remember these, remember that the notes spell "FACE."

Notes and Rests

Notes and rests are the building blocks of sheet music. These symbols indicate when to play (notes) and when to remain silent (rests).

- **Whole Note:** A solid circle without a stem represents a whole note. This note is held for the full duration of the note's value, usually lasting four beats in 4/4 time, standard time signature.

- **Half Note:** A half note looks like a whole note but has an upward stem. It is held for half the duration of a whole note, typically two beats in 4/4 time.

- **Quarter Note:** A quarter note is similar to a half note but has a filled-in circle with a stem. It is held for one-fourth the duration of a whole note, usually lasting one beat in 4/4 time.

- **Eighth Note:** An eighth note is distinguished by a filled-in circle with a stem and a flag. It is held for one-eighth the duration of a whole note, often taking half a beat in 4/4 time.

- **Rests:** Rests are symbols that indicate moments of silence in the music. They match the values of notes. For instance, a quarter rest corresponds to the silence duration of a quarter note, lasting one beat in 4/4 time.

Time Signatures and Rhythm

Time signatures play a crucial role in dictating the rhythm of a piece of music. They tell you how many beats are in each measure and which note receives one beat. Standard time signatures include 4/4 (four beats per measure, with a quarter note receiving one beat) and 3/4 (three beats per measure, with a quarter note receiving one beat).

Rhythmic patterns are created by combining different note durations within a measure. When you read music, tap your foot to the beat and count the rhythm aloud to internalize the timing of the music. For example, in 4/4 time, you'd typically count "1, 2, 3, 4" for each measure, with each number corresponding to a beat.

Reading and interpreting sheet music for the Trombone is a foundational skill every aspiring trombonist must develop. By understanding the staff, clefs, notes, key signatures, and time signatures, you can unlock the melodies hidden within those musical notations.

Developing a Sense of Rhythm and Musical Phrasing

Playing melodies isn't just about hitting the right notes but infusing them with rhythm and musical expression.

Metronome Practice

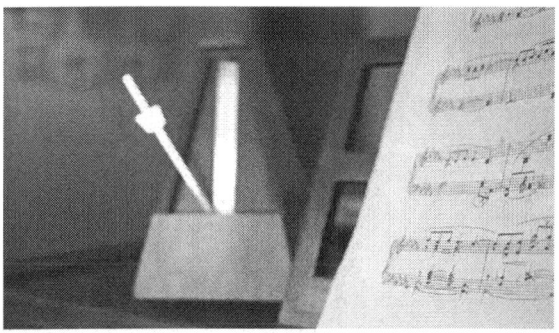

20. A metronome can help you develop a steady sense of rhythm.
Source:
https://unsplash.com/photos/EjmcTo9e3Jg?utm_source=unsplash
&utm_medium=referral&utm_content=creditShareLink

A metronome is an invaluable tool for developing a steady sense of rhythm. It provides a consistent beat to which you can align your playing. To use a metronome effectively:

1. **Select a Comfortable Tempo:** Start by setting your metronome to a comfortable tempo for the piece you're practicing.

2. **Tap Your Foot:** As you play along with the metronome, tap your foot to the beat. This physical connection helps you internalize the rhythm.

3. **Gradual Tempo Increases:** As you become more comfortable, gradually increase the tempo to challenge yourself. Practicing at different tempos will enhance your overall sense of rhythm.

4. **Subdividing Beats:** In more complex rhythms, it can be helpful to subdivide beats. For example, if you're in 4/4 time and the piece has eighth notes, you can count "1 and 2 and 3 and 4 and" to ensure precise timing.

Musical Phrasing

Phrasing is the art of shaping a melody to convey emotion and expression. It's what makes music come alive.

- **Dynamics:** Dynamics refers to the loudness and softness of notes. Pay attention to dynamic markings in the sheet music, such as "piano" (soft) and "forte" (loud). Experiment with crescendos (gradually getting louder) and decrescendos (gradually getting softer) to add expressive depth to your playing.

- **Articulation:** Articulation markings, such as staccato dots (short, detached notes) and legato lines (smooth, connected notes), guide your phrasing. Use these markings to contrast and highlight specific notes or phrases in the music.

- **Breath Control:** Use your breath to shape your phrases. Consider where to take breaths strategically to maintain a continuous flow of music. Experiment with different breath control techniques to achieve your desired phrasing.

- **Emotion:** Connect with the emotion of the music and convey it through your playing. Let your emotions guide your interpretation, whether it's joy, sadness, excitement, or tranquility. Tell a story through your Trombone, and let the music reflect your narrative.

- **Phrasing Markings:** Pay close attention to phrasing markings in the sheet music. These markings, such as slurs and phrase marks, indicate how the composer intended the music to be shaped. Follow these markings closely, but feel free to interpret them uniquely, adding your personal touch to the music.

Practice with Backing Tracks

Practice with backing tracks to enhance your sense of rhythm and musical phrasing. They are pre-recorded accompaniments that provide a musical context for your playing. Here's how to make the most of backing tracks:

- **Select Appropriate Tracks:** Choose backing tracks that align with the style and tempo of the piece you're practicing. You can find various backing tracks online, from classical to jazz to popular music.

- **Listen and Adapt:** Start by listening to the backing track without playing. Pay close attention to the music's rhythm, dynamics, and overall feel. It'll help you internalize the groove and style.

- **Play Along:** Once you're familiar with the backing track, start playing your Trombone along with it. Match your phrasing and timing to the track, creating a cohesive and engaging musical performance.

- **Experiment:** Don't be afraid to experiment with different interpretations. Use backing tracks as a creative tool to explore various phrasing options and rhythmic ideas, leading to exciting discoveries in your playing.

Congratulations! You can now play simple melodies on your Trombone. By applying techniques for breath control, lip slurs, and articulation, you can bring melodies to life. Understanding the basics of reading sheet music for the Trombone opens up a world of musical possibilities, and developing a sense of rhythm and musical phrasing allows you to express yourself through your playing.

As you continue your trombone journey, remember that practice is the key to mastery. Take the time to practice these techniques and immerse yourself in playing melodies. Seek out sheet music of varying complexities, from simple melodies to more challenging compositions. Embrace the joy of making music, and let your Trombone be your voice in the world of melodies and expression. Happy playing!

Chapter 8: Advancing Your Trombone Skills

Welcome to the final chapter of your trombone journey. By now, you've produced your first notes and started to play simple melodies. The world of trombone music is vast, and there's always room for growth and exploration.

In this chapter, you'll explore how to take your trombone skills to the next level and continue evolving as a musician. You'll uncover setting personal goals, track your progress, and delve into more complex musical pieces and genres. You'll find invaluable tips for continuous improvement. So prepare to elevate your Trombone playing to new heights.

Setting Personal Goals and Tracking Progress

*21. Setting goals is the first step towards improvement. Source:
https://unsplash.com/photos/LNzuOK1GxRU?utm_source=unsplas
h&utm_medium=referral&utm_content=creditShareLink*

Setting personal goals is the first step towards continuous improvement as a trombonist. Goals provide direction and motivation, helping you stay focused and inspired on your musical journey.

Goal Setting

- **Define Clear Objectives:** Define what you want to achieve with your Trombone playing. Is it mastering a specific technique, performing a challenging piece, or joining a musical ensemble? Be as specific as possible.

- **Short-Term and Long-Term Goals:** Create a mix of short-term and long-term goals. Short-term goals could be daily or weekly targets, while long-term goals may span several months or even years.

- **Realistic and Achievable:** Ensure your goals are realistic and attainable. Setting overly ambitious goals always leads to frustration. It's okay to challenge yourself, but make sure your goals are within reach.

- **Measurable Goals:** Make your goals measurable so you can track your progress. For instance, to improve your technical proficiency, set a goal to play a particular scale at a specific tempo.

- **Prioritize and Sequence:** Determine how you'll work on your goals. Some goals may be prerequisites for others. Prioritizing and sequencing your goals ensures a structured approach to improvement.

Tracking Progress

- **Keep a Practice Journal:** Maintain a journal to record your daily or weekly practice sessions. Note your achievements, areas that need improvement, and any challenges you encounter. This journal is a tool for self-assessment.

- **Use Technology:** Embrace technology to aid your progress tracking. Some apps and software designed for musicians help you monitor your tempo, pitch accuracy, and more.

- **Record Yourself:** Recording your practice sessions or performances is an excellent way to assess your progress objectively. Listen critically to your recordings to identify areas for improvement.

- **Celebrate Milestones:** When you achieve a goal, celebrate it. Whether playing a challenging piece flawlessly or mastering a new technique, acknowledging your achievements keeps you motivated.

- **Adjust and Adapt:** As you progress, be flexible with your goals. Sometimes, your musical interests or priorities evolve, and adjusting your goals is okay.

When you have a clear idea of where you want to go with your Trombone playing and you track your progress regularly, the possibilities are infinite. You'll feel more empowered as a musician and enjoy the improvement process. This is the first step in advancing your trombone skills.

Exploring More Complex Musical Pieces and Genres

Once you've mastered the basics, it's time to explore more complex musical pieces and genres. Diversifying your repertoire broadens your musical horizons and challenges you to grow as a player.

Expanding Your Repertoire

- **Classical Music:** If you haven't already, venture into the rich world of classical trombone music. Explore compositions by renowned composers like Mozart, Beethoven, and Brahms. Gradually tackle more complex pieces, such as orchestral excerpts or solo works.

- **Jazz and Contemporary Styles:** Jazz offers a unique avenue for trombonists. Familiarize yourself with jazz standards and improvisation. Study the works of jazz legends like J.J. Johnson and Slide Hampton. Don't shy away from contemporary styles, such as funk, fusion, and Latin jazz, which can be equally rewarding to explore.

- **Chamber Music:** Join or form a chamber music ensemble. Playing in a small group setting, whether a brass quintet or a brass choir, allows you to refine your ensemble skills and work closely with other musicians.

- **Solo Repertoire:** Challenge yourself with a solo repertoire composed explicitly for the Trombone. Pieces like the "Concertino for Trombone" by David R. Gillingham or the "Blue Bells of Scotland" by Arthur Pryor offer technical and musical challenges.

Continuous Learning

- **Music Theory:** Strengthen your music theory knowledge. Understanding harmony, chord progressions, and scales will deepen your musical understanding and improve your ability to interpret complex pieces.

- **Ear Training:** Develop your ear by practicing interval recognition, sight singing, and transcribing melodies. A well-trained ear is a valuable asset for any musician.

- **Advanced Techniques:** Explore advanced playing techniques, such as multiphonics, glissandos, and pedal tones. These techniques add unique colors and textures to your playing.

- **Mentorship:** Seek mentorship from experienced trombonists or musicians in your desired genre. Learning from those who have walked the path before you can provide invaluable insights and guidance.

The sky's the limit when it comes to advancing your trombone skills. Whether you're taking on a new genre or mastering advanced techniques, challenge yourself and explore the possibilities. With dedication and persistence, you'll be surprised by how far you can go with your Trombone playing.

Seeking Guidance from Teachers and Mentors

Regardless of your skill level, seeking guidance from teachers and mentors can accelerate your growth as a trombonist. Their expertise and feedback help you overcome challenges and refine your technique.

- **Private Lessons:** Consider taking private lessons with an experienced trombone instructor. Private lessons offer personalized guidance tailored to your specific needs and goals. Your teacher can identify areas for improvement, provide constructive feedback, and offer exercises and repertoire recommendations.

- **Music Teachers and Professors:** If you're a student or aspiring to pursue music academically, consider enrolling in a music program or conservatory. Music teachers and professors can provide comprehensive trombone performance, music theory, and history education.

- **Mentorship:** Mentorship is a valuable resource for trombonists at all levels. Establishing a mentorship relationship with an experienced player can provide ongoing support and guidance. Mentors offer career advice, share performance opportunities, and help you navigate the music industry.

- **Online Resources:** Besides in-person guidance, take advantage of online resources. Numerous trombone tutorials, masterclasses, and forums are available on the internet. Websites like YouTube offer many instructional videos on various aspects of trombone playing. For example, the page Basicband on YouTube features videos on tone production, breathing exercises, and improvisation.

You don't have to go it alone as a trombonist. Taking advantage of the resources available and seeking guidance from teachers and mentors will help you progress quickly and confidently. If you're looking to advance your trombone skills, don't be afraid to reach out and ask for help. It's a great way to grow as a musician. With the right resources and guidance, the sky is the limit when advancing your trombone skills.

Tips for Continuous Improvement and Honing Your Skills

Continuous improvement is the key to becoming an accomplished trombonist. Here are some tips to help you stay on the path of growth and excellence:

- **Consistent Practice:** Maintain a regular practice routine. Daily practice, even for a short duration, is more effective than occasional lengthy sessions. Consistency builds muscle memory and skill retention.

- **Warm-Up and Maintenance:** Begin each practice session with a proper warm-up to prevent injury and ensure your embouchure is ready. Regularly clean and maintain your instrument to optimize its performance.

- **Explore New Techniques:** Don't shy away from challenging techniques and styles. Embrace the unfamiliar and incorporate it into your practice routine.

- **Attend Workshops and Clinics:** Participate in workshops and clinics led by experienced trombonists. These events offer opportunities for hands-on learning and networking with fellow musicians.

- **Stay Inspired:** Attend live performances, listen to a wide range of music, and read about trombone history and musicians. Staying inspired and curious about your instrument keeps your passion alive.

- **Teach Others:** Teaching can deepen your understanding of music and technique. Consider offering lessons to beginners or mentoring younger musicians.

Resources for Advancing Your Trombone Skills

Advancing your trombone skills is an exciting journey, and there are plenty of valuable resources to help you along the way.

Online Forums

- **Trombone Forum (trombone.org):** This vibrant online community is a hub for trombonists of all levels. It's a fantastic place to read reviews, find news, and connect with fellow enthusiasts.

- **Reddit - r/Trombone (reddit.com/r/Trombone):** Reddit offers a dedicated space for trombone players. You can find discussions on technique and gear and share your experiences here.

Publications

- **"The Art of Trombone Playing" by Edward Kleinhammer:** This classic book is a must-read for any serious trombonist. It delves deep into the nuances of playing and offers valuable insights into tone production and technique.

- **Trombone Method by Troy "Trombone Shorty" Andrews:** This is a fantastic method book by the renowned trombonist Trombone Shorty. It covers various playing styles and techniques, making it suitable for beginners and advanced players.

Online Communities

- **Trombone Chat (trombonechat.com):** This online community hosts discussions on various trombone-related topics, and it's an excellent place to connect with experienced players.

- **Facebook Groups:** Search for trombone-related groups on Facebook. There are numerous communities where you can share your progress, ask for advice, and stay updated on trombone news.

Sheet Music Libraries

- **IMSLP (International Music Score Library Project) (imslp.org):** IMSLP is a public domain sheet music treasure trove, including classical pieces perfect for honing your skills.

- **J.W. Pepper (jwpepper.com):** This site offers a wide selection of sheet music for trombone players, ranging from classical to contemporary pieces.

Trombone Associations

- **International Trombone Association (ITA) (trombone.net):** ITA provides a wealth of resources, including publications, competitions, and a network of professional trombonists.

- **British Trombone Society (britishtrombonesociety.org):** If you're in the

UK, this association offers support, events, and a vibrant community of trombonists.

Remember, advancing your trombone skills is a gradual process. Explore these resources, engage with the community, and practice consistently. Whether you want to improve your technique, discover new music, or connect with fellow trombonists, these resources will guide your musical journey.

Congratulations on finishing the final chapter of your trombone journey. Growth as a trombonist is a lifelong journey. Embrace challenges, stay curious, and let your passion for music guide you. Your Trombone will continue to be a source of joy, expression, and personal fulfillment as you advance your skills and make beautiful music. Keep playing, keep learning, and keep reaching for the stars.

Conclusion

Congratulations. You are now on a journey to master the art of playing the Trombone. Throughout this book, you've explored a comprehensive guide that has taken you from a complete novice to a budding trombonist. Here are the key takeaways from each of the chapters to reinforce your learning:

Chapter 1: Background to the Trombone

- **Historical Significance:** The Trombone has a rich history dating back centuries. Understanding its origins and evolution will deepen your appreciation for this remarkable instrument.

- **Variety of Trombones:** Trombones come in various types and sizes, each with its unique sound and purpose. Familiarize yourself with these variations to choose the right one for your musical journey.

- **Versatility:** The Trombone's versatility allows it to shine in various musical genres, from classical to jazz and beyond. Embrace this versatility as you explore your musical interests.

Chapter 2: Getting to Know Your Instrument

- **Trombone Anatomy:** Knowing the parts of your instrument is crucial. Understanding the slide, bell, mouthpiece, and more will set you up for success.

- **Proper Maintenance:** Regular maintenance ensures your Trombone stays in optimal condition. Cleanliness and proper care will extend its lifespan and maintain its tonal quality.

- **Tuning and Pitch:** Learning how to tune your Trombone is essential for harmonizing with other musicians. Mastering pitch adjustment is a valuable skill.

Chapter 3: The Basics of Trombone Playing

- **Posture and Positioning:** Proper posture and positioning lay the foundation for playing the Trombone effectively. Pay attention to your body's alignment to avoid strain and discomfort.

- **Breathing Techniques:** Breathing is the engine of your Trombone playing. Understanding diaphragmatic breathing and breath control is crucial for sustaining notes and phrases.

- **Basic Notation:** Familiarize yourself with musical notation, including notes, rests, and time signatures. This knowledge will help you read and interpret music.

Chapter 4: Proper Embouchure and Breath Control

- **Embouchure Mastery:** Your embouchure, or how you shape your lips and use your facial muscles, dramatically affects your tone. Practice and refine your embouchure to produce precise, resonant notes.

- **Breath Support:** Building robust breath control is essential. Incorporate exercises and techniques to develop the ability to play longer phrases and maintain consistent sound.

- **Warm-Up Routine:** Establish a warm-up routine to prepare your body and mind for playing. Warm-up exercises enhance your performance and reduce the risk of injury.

Chapter 5: Producing Your First Notes

- **Making a Sound:** The moment you produce your first sound on the Trombone is exhilarating. Remember that patience and perseverance are your allies in this journey.

- **Tone Quality:** Focus on achieving a clear and pleasant tone. Listen to your sound and make subtle adjustments to refine your playing.

- **Intervals and Scales:** To build your musical vocabulary, begin exploring intervals and scales. This knowledge will become invaluable as you progress.

Chapter 6: Learning Basic Techniques

- **Articulation:** Mastering different articulation techniques, such as legato and staccato, adds depth and expressiveness to your playing.

- **Slide Techniques:** The slide is your unique tool as a trombonist. Learn how to maneuver it smoothly to hit the right notes and create beautiful glissandos.

- **Dynamic Control:** Practice dynamic changes from soft pianissimo to powerful fortissimo. These variations in volume add emotion and drama to your music.

Chapter 7: Playing Simple Melodies

- **Melodic Interpretation:** Bring melodies to life by infusing your personal style and emotion into your playing. Remember, music is not just notes. It's a language of feelings.

- **Rhythmic Precision:** Develop your sense of rhythm. Precise timing and rhythm are essential for playing melodies with accuracy.

- **Listening and Ensemble Playing:** Start playing with others. Listening and collaborating with fellow musicians will enhance your musicality and ensemble skills.

Chapter 8: Advancing Your Trombone Skills

- **Continual Learning:** The journey of a trombonist is ongoing. Explore new techniques, genres, and musical styles to expand your horizons.

- **Solo and Performance:** Consider solo performances or joining ensembles to showcase your talent. Confidence in performing will grow with experience.

- **Review and Share:** Share your progress and experiences with others. Ask for feedback from teachers, peers, or online communities to refine your skills.

Your dedication and hard work have brought you to this point in your trombone journey. Always remember that learning an instrument is a lifelong pursuit, and the joy of playing music is a gift that keeps on giving. Continue practicing, exploring, and sharing your musical talents with the world.

If you could take a moment to leave a review of this book, your feedback will improve and inspire more aspiring trombonists on their musical voyage. Thank you for choosing "How to Play the Trombone for Beginners," and may your musical endeavors bring you endless joy and fulfillment.

References

Allard, B. [@bryantallard1890]. (2016, December 30). Reading Notes Trombone. Youtube. https://www.youtube.com/watch?v=tsTG0dpCXNo

Beginners guide to learning the Trombone. (n.d.). Ted's List. https://teds-list.com/beginners-guide/beginners-guide-to-learning-the-trombone/

Gee, M. (2022, February 7). How to read bass clef for Trombone. Matthew Gee.

How to play the Trombone. (2005, October 21). WikiHow. https://www.wikihow.com/Play-the-Trombone

How to Play the Trombone:How to play the Trombone - Musical Instrument Guide - Yamaha Corporation. (n.d.). Yamaha.com. https://www.yamaha.com/en/musical_instrument_guide/trombone/play/

Trombone for Beginners - Lesson 1. (n.d.). Sophia. https://app.sophia.org/tutorials/trombone-for-beginners-lesson-1

Printed in Great Britain
by Amazon